Paula
Danziger

Other titles in the *Authors Teens Love* series:

Ray Bradbury
Master of Science Fiction and Fantasy
0-7660-2240-4

Orson Scott Card
Architect of Alternate Worlds
0-7660-2354-0

Roald Dahl
Author of Charlie and the Chocolate Factory
0-7660-2353-2

C. S. Lewis
Chronicler of Narnia
0-7660-2446-6

Joan Lowery Nixon
Masterful Mystery Writer
0-7660-2194-7

R. L. Stine
Creator of Creepy and Spooky Stories
0-7660-2445-8

J. R. R. Tolkien
Master of Imaginary Worlds
0-7660-2246-3

E. B. White
Spinner of Webs and Tales
0-7660-2350-8

AUTHORS TEENS LOVE

Paula Danziger

Voice of Teen Troubles

Jennifer Bond Reed

Enslow Publishers, Inc.
40 Industrial Road
Box 398
Berkeley Heights, NJ 07922
USA
http://www.enslow.com

Library of Congress Cataloging-in-Publication Data

Reed, Jennifer.
    Paula Danziger : voice of teen troubles / Jennifer Bond Reed.
        p. cm. — (Authors teens love)
    Includes bibliographical references and index.
    ISBN 0-7660-2444-X
    1. Danziger, Paula—Juvenile literature. 2. Authors, American—
20th century—Biography—Juvenile literature. 3. Young adult fiction—
Authorship—Juvenile literature. 4. Teenagers—Books and reading—
Juvenile literature. I. Title. II. Series.
    PS3554.A585Z85 2006
    813'.54—dc22

                              2005030332

Printed in the United States of America

10 9 8 7 6 5 4 3 2 1

To Our Readers: We have done our best to make sure all Internet address-
es in this book were active and appropriate when we went to press.
However, the author and publisher have no control over and assume no lia-
bility for the material available on those Internet sites or on other Web sites
they may link to. Any comments or suggestions can be sent by e-mail to
comments@enslow.com or to the address on the back cover.

Illustration Credits: All interior photos courtesy of Barry Danziger,
except p. 6, courtesy of Linda Singleton; and p. 13, Nina
Rosenstein / Enslow Publishers, Inc.

Cover Illustration: Courtesy of Barry Danziger (photo), and Mark
A. Hicks (background art).

Contents

Evelyn Gallardo

Chapter 1

Funny Girl

Flamboyant, funny, inspirational, showy, a hypochondriac, kind, talented, giving, and deeply honest. These are just some of the words people have used to describe Paula Danziger. She was one of a kind. Danziger was full of life. She loved people, and everywhere she went she focused on getting to know them.

Paula Danziger also loved clothes, especially shoes. She collected them as well as purses. Danziger would often show up at schools for a presentation wearing sequined tennis sneakers. At writer's conferences, she might appear in flashy cowboy boots. Her favorite color was purple—a rich, vibrant color that matched Danziger's personality. People were drawn to her first, perhaps because of her flamboyant dress, but soon because they realized she was a kind and giving person.

Eileen Spinelli, children's author, remembered Paula Danziger painting her fingernails with purple sparkle nail polish at a writer's conference.[1] Danziger had flair from her head to her toes. Often she would wrap a scarf around her head, like a crown. Big bold rings adorned her fingers, which she would flutter for all to see. She loved jewelry too. The bigger, the brighter, the better. However, it was not what she wore that caught the attention of her teen fans. It was how she related to them in her writing.

Paula Danziger had some help. Not only did she use her own childhood experiences in her books, but she also received help from her family. Sam Danziger, one of Paula's nephews (she had three nephews and a niece), often traveled with his aunt. "Paula was always most concerned with the people we met; this was always what was interesting to her."[2]

Danziger enjoyed traveling. She took her nephews and niece on many trips. Sam thought that his aunt wanted to get his family out of the small town where they lived in New Jersey, to see the world. Sam recalled that, "No matter where we were, the place we were at was just a backdrop."[3] Danziger was a people person. People influenced her in many ways and she created delightful characters inspired by the people she met.

The world may never have known Paula Danziger if it were not for two serious car

Some of Paula Danziger's flashy footwear, painted and decorated by the famous author herself.

accidents in the same month in 1970. While she was stopped at a stop sign, a police car came up from behind and pushed her car into an intersection. She suffered whiplash, which was painful, but she did not suffer any other serious injuries.

Then, just six days later, she was hit by a drunk driver. Danziger was hit head-on. Wearing a seat belt saved her life, but her head crashed into the windshield. Danziger says she had one hundred stitches in her face. Shortly after her accidents, she began having problems. Danziger found it hard to read and then, like Leonardo da Vinci, she started writing backward. She could write in reverse! A brain scan showed that she had suffered brain damage but how much was not known. Suddenly Paula Danziger's life turned upside down.

Once an independent woman living on her own, Danziger had to retreat to her parents' home to recover. This was not easy for a number of reasons, but during this stay, feelings about her childhood surfaced. Danziger began writing her first book, *The Cat Ate My Gymsuit*, as part of her recovery.[4] She did receive help from a dear friend, Maria Schantz, who was part of the department of Literacy and Educational Media at Montclair State College. Danziger adored her, and Maria encouraged her to realize her ambition to become a famous writer.[5]

Fans of Paula Danziger can only speculate that had it not been for the two car accidents, she would not have written *The Cat Ate My Gymsuit* and gone on to be a best-selling author. Fate favored her in the years to follow.

According to Danziger, her childhood was not easy. Her family was dysfunctional, a word commonly used today, but as Danziger said, "We were just Danzigers."[6] She had a hard time relating to her father who never hit, but he yelled a lot. Sometimes verbal abuse can be worse than physical abuse, and the trauma it caused Danziger over her lifetime was often written about in her books. "When my father would yell at me, I'd tell myself, 'Someday I'll use this in a book.'"[7]

Later in life, she was able to joke about her family saying, "We were a nuclear family only in the sense of being explosive."[8] Still, she loved her parents and her younger brother, Barry. She wrote to sort out her own problems in life and to connect with both teens and children on a very new and different level.

When Danziger's first book was published in 1974, there were several writers whose books were also making their way into the hands of teen readers. Judy Blume, S. E. Hinton, and Richard Peck, just to name a few, were emerging teen authors. The early seventies was a time of cultural and social change. Book publishing was not immune.

Judy Blume said in an interview with *Writer's Digest* that, "In the early '70s—a very good time for children's books and their authors—editors and publishers were willing to take a chance on a new writer. They were willing and able to invest their time in nurturing writers with promise, encouraging them."[9] Today, many editors just do not have the time to spend with new writers, and breaking into the teen market can be difficult. Danziger entered the scene with a book that dealt with a lot of problems people just did not talk about—eating disorders, self-esteem, and verbal abuse. Editors paid attention to what she wrote because readers loved her. Danziger enjoyed writing and was willing to take a chance with *The Cat Ate My Gymsuit*. It was the most autobiographical book she would ever write, and teens across America loved it.

Paula Danziger dealt with tough issues through humor. Her book was "deeply honest" and poignant, but also very funny. Danziger liked to tell jokes and be funny. Therefore, it is only natural that her beloved characters would also deal with life through humor. The young protagonist in *The Cat Ate My Gymsuit* is filled with angst early on in the story. She is having a hard time coping with family, her life, and her body:

"My four year old brother wants to be my best friend so I can help him put orange pits in a hole in his teddy bear's head."

"I'm flat-chested. I used to buy training bras and put tucks in them."[10]

What thirteen-year-old girl could not relate to the humor? Danziger knew what would catch her readers' attention. For young teen girls, finding independence from family and body development

> **My four year old brother wants to be my best friend so I can help him put orange pits in a hole in his teddy bear's head. I'm flat-chested. I used to buy training bras and put tucks in them.**

was as important in 1970 as it is in the 21st century.

Some people wonder why Paula Danziger did not become a stand-up comedian. She had no inhibitions and easily spoke to a crowd. Not only did she love sharing her books and ideas, but she liked

Danziger signs copies of *Amber Brown Sees Red* at an American Library Association (ALA) conference in San Francisco in July 1997.

to share her life—the good, the bad, and the ugly. "I tell more than most," she once said.[11]

Danziger was not afraid to share herself with a crowd of teenagers, children, and adults. After a writing conference, she had been known to take the stage at a restaurant and sing, causing the crowd to go into an uproar of laughter. Danziger was one of the funniest people she knew and did not mind admitting this.[12] She loved to make people laugh. As her good friend and fellow children's author Bruce Coville said, "She was funny, just because she was funny! She loved humor."[13]

13

Danziger never made light of a serious subject. She wanted to show people that despite the tough times and hardships, humor and laughter could make life bearable. From the titles of her books, like *The Cat Ate My Gymsuit*, *Make Like a Tree and Leave*, and *Can You Sue Your Parents for Malpractice?*, to her amusing and real-to-life characters such as Marcy Lewis, Matthew Martin, and Lauren Allen, Danziger instilled humor. In fact, the last names of her famous protagonists all come from famous comedians: Jerry Lewis, Dean Martin, and Woody Allen. Her book titles always cause people to stop, ponder, and smile.

> **She wanted to show people that despite the tough times and hardships, humor and laughter could make life bearable.**

Danziger stood out among authors because she deeply understood what it was like to be a teenager. She stood out because she made people think and laugh. What was funny twenty years ago is often still funny today. Danziger knew that humor in her books would be timeless. She wrote good stories with memorable characters that teen readers could relate to over the generations. She wrote about her own problems, and how she handled them. "I don't come down to kids' level," she said.

"I respond on a level I feel comfortable on." A teen perspective usually happens to be the same as hers.[14]

Some people would say that Paula Danziger never grew up. Most agree she never lost her unique ability to think like a teenager.

Knowing she wanted to be a writer since she was seven years old, Paula Danziger fulfilled her dream in huge ways. With over thirty books to her credit, including the popular Amber Brown series and her first and only picture book, *Barfburger Baby, I Was Here First*, published in September 2004, Paula Danziger became one of the most beloved teen and children's authors in the 21st century.

Chapter 2

A Writer Is Born

The world was in turmoil in 1943. America was at war and men were being drafted to fight overseas. Samuel Danziger was enlisted in the Army. One night at a USO canteen in Washington, D.C., he met the woman he would marry, Carolyn Siegel. Samuel was from the Bronx, New York, and Carolyn was from Queens. The two came from similar backgrounds.[1] They fell in love and were soon married.

Paula Danziger was born on August 18, 1944, in Washington, D.C. Although an exciting event for Carolyn Danziger, an important family member was missing: Paula's father. Samuel Danziger was stationed in Honolulu, Hawaii, and received word of the birth of his daughter via telegraph. Paula was the first child born to Carolyn and Samuel

Danziger. Her mother sent word, "Daughter born please don't worry. Greetings from all of us."[2]

Samuel Danziger replied, "Received news of birth of daughter. I wish we were together on this special occasion. All my best for a speedy reunion. Love. Samuel Danziger."[3]

The absence of Paula's father from the very beginning was perhaps just the precursor of an emotionally absent father. Paula's father returned eighteen months later. He hardly knew the baby girl he had helped to create. From Washington, the family moved to New Jersey.

Paula's memories of her childhood and the family unit were different from those of her brother, Barry. Barry was born in New Jersey. Paula remembers a home filled with tension—much of it stemming from her father. According to Paula, he was "ruler of the roost" and everything he said was the law. If you disagreed with him, he would yell and demean you.[4] Paula was mad at her mother, too, because her mother never stood up to him. Paula's father worked in the garment industry and her mother was trained as a nurse. When they had children, Danziger's mother chose to stay at home.

The relationship between a parent and child is often difficult. Paula wanted to be close to her father. She yearned for that special relationship between a father and daughter. It was not meant to be. This is not to say that Samuel Danziger did not love Paula. Her brother, Barry, believed he did. He just did not show it in ways that Paula needed.

Barry's relationship with his parents was quite

Paula Danziger's parents, Samuel and Carolyn, in 1943.

different; partly because he was a boy and partly because he seemed to understand his parents better. Barry had a stronger relationship with his mother. Barry recalled, "I did not let my father get to me. I realized where he was coming from. I walked away most of the time—even though I was [angry]. Paula let the whole world know she was being persecuted."[5]

Barry Danziger understood that his father did not grow up with a lot of affection. Therefore, his father had a hard time showing it. He worked very hard and spent most of his time at his job. Paula often overreacted to different situations. "She never learned how to handle solutions and adversity, she took everything personally. As a result, she overreacted when my father would do anything she thought might be a slight."[6]

Paula recognized later in life that her father did not have an easy childhood. Both parents were first-generation immigrants from Poland. They escaped prior to World War II to America. Many family members left behind were put in concentration camps. Paula recalled that "even his father's mother was not crazy about him . . . he wasn't well treated. . . . His was a family that did not show love easily."[7]

Barry Danziger commented that both his parents would speak Yiddish when they did not want to include Paula or him in their discussions. This frustrated both Paula and Barry and made them angry, but also, Barry believes it is the reason neither of them liked foreign languages.[8]

By the time Paula was twelve years old she was in serious trouble. The anxiety from her family situation and inability to cope with it caused anger. Paula turned this anger onto herself. "At age 12, I was put on tranquilizers when I should have gotten help. There was nothing major and awful, I just didn't feel [my family] was supportive and emotionally generous. My father was a very unhappy person, very sarcastic, and my mother was very nervous and worried about what people thought. They weren't monsters, but it wasn't a good childhood."[9]

Paula became bulimic. This psychological

Paula at age five, outside the family home in Nutley, New Jersey.

eating disorder mainly affects girls. It involves a compulsive pattern of binge eating and then purging the food to get rid of the weight. For some it involves throwing up, use of laxatives, and fasting.[10] For Paula, she chose to throw up the food she had eaten. Binge eating and purging does not happen because a person is hungry. It is a response to issues such as depression, stress, or lack of self-esteem. Bulimics may also suffer from other problems such as stomach ruptures; troubles with the heart, kidneys, and liver; as well as dental problems. Paula's teeth were so bad that as an adult she had to have periodontal work done. Stomach acids destroy the enamel and require sometimes painful dental work to make the teeth healthy again. Bulimia was not diagnosed as an eating disorder until 1980.[11] Before that, doctors would only prescribe tranquilizers to their patients rather than deal with the emotional problems involved with the disorder.

Danziger admits that she did not binge and purge to lose weight, even though she always had a weight problem as a child. "It was something I did when I was most angry with myself."[12] People did not talk about eating disorders when Danziger was growing up. Her brother noted that their mother often pointed out how heavy they were. Even though Barry had lost 77 pounds between grades eleven and twelve, their mother's usual comment was that he would put it all back on.[13] There was little support at home.

That seemed to be a major problem for Paula Danziger. It took many years before she got treatment for bulimia. She insisted though that she did not want to be treated as a survivor of the disease. She wanted kids to know that with help, they can survive.[14]

Paula Danziger knew she wanted to be a writer ever since she was in the second grade. She busily created stories as a child. She loved books, and would spend countless hours at the library reading everything she could devour. Reading about other children with problems was an escape for Paula.

The Little Engine that Could was her first favorite book, and as Danziger said, "I still use that line, 'I think I can, I think I can, I know I can' before anything that makes me nervous—a speech or a big date or doing a TV show."[15]

As she got older, she enjoyed books written by Ray Bradbury and J. D. Salinger and the Nancy Drew and Hardy Boys books. Of course, she also enjoyed comics like Little LuLu, Jughead, and Veronica.[16] If it was printed, Paula read it. It is not surprising that Paula took this escape method from her own, real world a step further by creating her own characters and stories. For Paula, as with many authors, writing starts with a deep love for reading.

The school years for Paula were often not stimulating. She attended Metuchen High School in New Jersey. She talked a lot and often got into trouble for it. Paula also remembered that her classes did not encourage creative writing. She found creativity in other ways, including drama classes and as the art editor on the *Bulldog Bark*, the high school paper. Paula also joined the high school chorus because she loved to sing. When she was told to stop goofing around and start singing in her "real" voice, Paula dropped out. Writing, even then, was truly her strength.

When it was time for Paula to apply for colleges, her father quit his job and became a real estate agent. There was no money to send Paula to school, and this angered her. Paula received a scholarship to Montclair State Teacher's College, in Montclair, New Jersey. Her parents did help later, and she earned her bachelor's degree in English. In fact, her counselor at high school did not think she could even get in to Montclair. "He challenged me," recalled Danziger, who planned to major in speech therapy. "My mother wanted me to be a nurse, so I thought becoming a speech therapist was like being a nurse without the blood." However, she discovered she was not as good in science as she was working with adolescents. Paula turned to teaching.[17]

While at college, she was the editor of *Galumph*, the campus humor magazine. She often dreamed of becoming a rich and famous author, winning a Pulitzer prize.[18] She also played the glockenspiel her freshman year in the marching band during football season. This seemed odd to her brother, Barry, since she never had a lesson in her life.

A librarian in college introduced Paula to John Ciardi, a well-known poet. He was deeply connected to the academic world, lecturing at colleges, and doing poetry readings. He also wrote children's poetry. He greatly influenced Paula and her writing. Paula baby-sat for his children and soon he discovered her desire to write books. Ciardi and his wife took Paula to writer's conferences. "He taught me a lot about language," she remembers. He suggested that she analyze one

A childhood photo of Paula Danziger at about age six. Danziger's childhood experiences would color nearly all of her later writings as an adult.

poem by underlining the funny lines in red and the serious lines in blue. By the end of the poem, Ciardi said, you get purple—Paula's favorite color!

"That's what I always write toward," Danziger says, "that mixture."[19]

Paula Danziger went on to teach both junior and senior high school. She also learned how to act. Danziger felt that anyone interested in the craft of writing should take acting lessons. "They're wonderful for anyone who wants to learn about characterization and motivation."[20]

During this time, she got her master's degree in reading. She also taught at the college level. Danziger held many jobs, too, before she became a teacher. She worked as a playground supervisor, a gift wrapper at a department store, and as an assembly-line worker in a cosmetics factory. When she found success with *The Cat Ate My Gymsuit*, she decided to devote her time to writing. "The only other things I would consider doing now," says Danziger, "are being on television and stand-up comedy."[21]

Danziger did eventually have her own television show in England with the BBC, but writing was always her passion. Her first book published has sold millions of copies and is still in print, over thirty years later.

Chapter 3

A Believable Character

"Marcy Lewis in *The Cat Ate My Gymsuit* is the closest to who I am. If she were to grow up, she'd definitely be writing somewhere."[1]

Since the 1974 publication of her first novel, *The Cat Ate My Gymsuit*, Paula Danziger has become one of America's most popular authors for young adults. Most of her books "center around young teenage girls faced with the problems of establishing a grownup identity," as Alleen Pace Nilsen summarizes in *Twentieth-Century Children's Writers*.

But while Danziger's characters frequently deal with personal and family problems, they do so with humor, wit, and spirit. As a result, Nilsen writes, "teenagers begin to smile at themselves and come away from [Danziger's] books a little more confident that they too will make it."[2]

One of the most famous and controversial lines Paula Danziger ever wrote was the first line in *The Cat Ate My Gymsuit*, "I hate my father." Danziger writes from the viewpoint of thirteen-year-old Marcy Lewis. Marcy is full of disdain for her family, school, and life in general. She vented in the opening paragraph, "I hate my father. I hate school. I hate being fat. I hate the principal."[3]

Not only has Danziger set the tone for her first book, she also defines teen angst. It is not easy being a teenager. Danziger knew this firsthand. Like many kids, her teen years were difficult due to an eating disorder and a father to whom she could not relate. As Danziger claimed many times, *The Cat Ate My Gymsuit* was the closest she ever came to writing her autobiography.

Danziger knew that she wanted to be a writer, but it was not until two back-to-back car accidents that this dream became clear. The accidents caused physical problems, including dyslexia. Her recuperation was spent at home, with her mother and father. She was forced to take a hard look at her life and her family. What she saw was not what she wanted to see. She wanted reconciliation with her parents, and she wanted to write. Danziger began writing a story about a young girl, Marcy, who in many ways was just like Danziger. Marcy's dad was like Danziger's dad, or at least the way Danziger perceived her father. The relationship between Danziger and her dad bubbles over on the pages of *The Cat Ate My Gymsuit*. It seemed that Danziger found an outlet for her anxiety and problems at home, and at the same time, a way to touch the lives of millions of teens all over the world.

Family members had mixed feelings about *The Cat Ate My Gymsuit*. When Danziger handed a copy of the book to her parents, she told them that there were things in it that they would not like.[4] Danziger talked to her father in particular about it, and their relationship improved. Through her writing, Danziger learned to let go of her anger.

Sam Danziger loved his aunt dearly and admitted that he had only recently read *The Cat Ate My*

Paula Danziger as a young teenager with her Uncle Earl and Aunt Binin. Aunt Binin was to Paula like what Paula would be to her own niece, Carrie.

Gymsuit. "*Cat* was very valuable to me in that it helped me know my grandfather. It was also valuable in making me appreciate my aunt, her abilities as an author—she really was a very good writer."[5]

The main character in *Cat*, Marcy Lewis, lacks self-esteem. She compensates by overeating. Her father is unhappy at work and seems to feel better when he belittles others, especially Marcy. Marcy's little brother, Stuart, looks up to Marcy but seems scared. Scared of the yelling at home? Not feeling safe in a dysfunctional home? The reader does not really know, but Stuart acts out by stuffing his teddy bear full of orange pits (seeds). Marcy's mother never stands up to her husband. Marcy feels alone and angry, caught in the middle of her dysfunctional home.

Although Marcy can share her true feelings well, "I hate my father, I hate school," they are in fact a cover or excuse for the real problem she has yet to deal with. Marcy is afraid to come out of her protective shell, which simply keeps her bitter and unhappy.[6] Growing up is hard and full of physical and mental pain. Marcy does a lot of maturing in this story. She eventually learns that even though she is a teen, she has rights and a voice worthy of being heard. She comes out of her shell and helps Ms. Finney, her schoolteacher, fight a battle against authority and the establishment.

The Cat Ate My Gymsuit is not all gloomy. In fact, Danziger's humor shines throughout the book. This humor makes the book easy to read while covering some very serious teen issues. Marcy is coping with a tyrant of a father, being overweight, building her own self-confidence, and learning what it means to think for herself. She *is* Paula Danziger, and Danziger admittedly wrote the book as part of a recovery process. It seems that Danziger was trying to recover from a difficult childhood dealing with being overweight and having low self esteem. She was also trying to cope with her relationship with her own father who is represented by the book's father, Martin Lewis. So when she writes, "I hate my father," the reader feels the anger that still swelled inside of Paula Danziger.

Of course, it is easy to see why Marcy hates her father. Throughout the book, he is quick to criticize. He does not support her. He calls her "young lady" in a derogatory way and he yells. Short of being physically violent, Martin Lewis is verbally abusive. When he sends Marcy to her room without dinner, he is quick to add, "That's alright. The girl won't waste away to nothing."[7] He also puts his wife down in front of the children and intimidates the entire family. He feels that he does enough by working hard and supporting his family financially. Danziger based Marcy's parents on her own, just as Marcy was like Paula. "I was much like that child; my parents were much like those parents."[8]

The Cat Ate My Gymsuit is a fiction piece but as Danziger said, "I wrote what I knew best. I was a fat little teenager from New Jersey who hated

Paula Danziger at approximately eighteen years old, in the backyard of her family's Metuchen home circa 1962.

school with a younger brother who stuck orange pits in his bear."[9]

Although Marcy is powerless to change her situation, she does a lot of growing up. Readers can easily identify with Marcy's problems and feelings as much today as when the book was first published in 1974. Marcy wants more control of her life, but independence does not come easy, as most teens realize.

When Ms. Finney is introduced in the book, she stands out from the rest of the adults who are continually telling Marcy what to do, what to feel, and what to think. Ms. Finney, the new English teacher, encourages her students to think for themselves and communicate with each other. Marcy discovers that communicating is the way she can find her way out of her troubles and free herself from the ever-controlling adults in her life. She is not powerless after all, and neither is Danziger, as she communicates her feelings and angst about her teen years and her father through Marcy.

The sequel to *The Cat Ate My Gymsuit* is *There's a Bat in Bunk Five*. Danziger's first book was a huge success and readers begged for a sequel. Nearly four years later, *There's a Bat in Bunk Five* was published. Marcy Lewis has come a long way and so has her family. Danziger wanted to show her readers that Marcy was a survivor. Marcy received counseling for her troubles at the end of *Cat*. In the beginning of *There's a Bat in Bunk Five*, Marcy is on her way to summer camp. She will be a counselor. Marcy is eager to be independent, to meet new friends, and to be with her old teacher from *Cat*, Ms. Finney.

Danziger got the idea to write this sequel about Marcy when her own students returned from summer camp. Danziger says, "It's a time when kids leave home, meet new people and try out new behavior." Danziger admitted that she had been to camp once before. "It was a complete disaster! One week after I got there, my mother became camp nurse and brought along my little brother. So much for getting away!"[10]

Marcy leaves home and leaves some of her problems behind. Danziger makes Marcy's experience at camp generally good. She is not the whiner she was in *Cat*. In fact, it is clear Marcy has a different attitude.

In the beginning, Marcy has lost weight and convinced her dad to let her go to camp. Their relationship is still full of tension, but Marcy has addressed some feelings about her father. She tells the reader how her dad had a heart attack at the beginning of the summer. She admits, "I get scared he is going to die."[11] But the tension comes back when in the next line she says, "Sometimes I wish he were dead, I hate him so much. But there's a part of me that really loves him."[12]

Marcy's confusion about her own feelings is evident. Once her parents leave the camp after dropping her off, Marcy realizes it is time to be Marcy.

She learns a lot about herself at camp. As a camp counselor, Marcy is responsible for a group of girls. She eats, sleeps, and works with them, making sure their camp experience is good. The girls are different. They come from different areas and social backgrounds, but one, Ginger, seems more difficult than the others. Although Marcy is determined to help Ginger, everything she tries fails. Ginger, a child of divorce, is too much for anyone at camp. Marcy's "savior" attitude is much like Danziger's. "Kids who feel alone sometimes think there's a chance when they meet someone like me. I reach the outlaws, the lurkers."[13] The outlaw, Ginger, is not reached by Marcy. She sees that other people do have it worse than she does.

Marcy also has her first boyfriend at camp. Her romantic experience with Ted is appropriate for the teen audience. The romance itself is very naïve, but Marcy is able to experience the affections of someone from the opposite sex. She experiences her first kiss and all the emotions that go with liking a boy. Danziger handles the issues well, relating them to a teen audience. Although Marcy is more mature, there are some hilarious moments throughout that remind readers that this is the same beloved Marcy from *Cat*.

While on a date with Ted in a local town, Marcy realizes something terrible is happening. "All of a sudden, I feel something weird around my hips, under my skirt. It's my panty hose. They're starting to roll down."[14] Marcy is forced to tell Ted what is happening and they have a good laugh. "I imagine what it would have been like to have my panty hose roll down to my ankles in front of everyone. It's too awful to even think about."[15]

Bat is the first book Danziger wrote as a full-time writer. Danziger came to the realization that it was hard to be a good creative writer and a good creative teacher at the same time. "Each was a full-time job. My choice was to write full time. I was never good at taking attendance, doing lesson plans, or getting papers back on time. I sold two ideas to Dell, took the advance money, and hoped for decent royalties."[16] She was scared and had some anxiety attacks. Switching careers was risky, and she knew she would miss her students. "I miss working with the kids, but I don't miss the faculty meetings, taking attendance, and grading papers," Danziger revealed. "I'm also not great about getting papers back in time. My strength as a teacher was that I really cared about kids, books and creativity."[17]

Would her new book be a success? Would the critics like the new Marcy? Could she survive as a full-time writer? Although these questions sometimes plagued Danziger, she focused on the new Marcy and her summer experience.

Marcy, like Danziger had a lot of questions about her future. What will happen to Ginger? What will happen between Marcy and Ted? How will her parents react to the more grown-up Marcy? Life is full of questions that do not always get answered and Marcy is fine with that. She does not want camp to end, but she also wants to get home—"To experience new things."[18]

The last sentences reflect Danziger's own attitude toward life. She and Marcy have dealt with a lot and both survived. "It's kind of like what I've thought, that my life goes on like a novel with lots of character development. But there is change. There is a plot.

"I can hardly wait for the next chapter."[19]

Chapter 4

Real Life in Fiction

*P*aula Danziger never wanted to write stories with messages, yet all of her books contain them. She felt that if she wrote with the intention of sending a message, her writing would seem preachy. So she wrote about life and told stories the best way she could. She wrote from experience, about the people she met, and she wrote from her heart.

Several books dealing with life as a teenager come to mind. *The Pistachio Prescription, Can You Sue Your Parents for Malpractice? Divorce Express,* and *It's an Ardvaark-Eat-Turtle World* all have young teens for the main character. All have problems that many teens face daily: fitting in, divorce, friendships, eating problems, weight issues, self-worth, just to name a few.

But even though Danziger wrote about teens,

one subject she would not touch was sex. Her family knew this as well, according to her nephew, Sam. "Aunt said she found the idea of serious dating and her characters having sex very distasteful. I suppose even she couldn't find anything funny about puberty."[1] She did admit this as well. The more serious issues involving teens today—sex, teen shootings, and drug abuse—were beyond Danziger. She felt that there were better writers to write on these subjects than herself. "None of my characters seems to have had sex yet—I haven't written about that. And I wouldn't want to deal with what's happening in Oregon—the school shootings. I'm never going to write that book. The way I see it, people like Robert Cormier are wonderful writers who cover those subjects. But I couldn't do them justice."[2] This does not mean she did not take on serious issues. "I made the choice long ago to write about real life. And life is both serious and funny."[3]

The Pistachio Prescription is similar to *Cat* but also quite different. This was Danziger's second book. At the time Danziger was writing this book, she was dealing with anger toward her mother. This is reflected through the main character, Cassie, who, like Marcy in *Cat*, lacks self-confidence. Cassie has other problems too, that include hypochondria and an addiction to pistachio nuts. These problems were not unique to Cassie. They were Danziger's problems too. The cause of Cassie's problems was not the father as it was in *Cat*; it was her mother.

Danziger remembered how difficult it was to fit in growing up. Whether it was in school or even at home, her mother was often critical. Danziger knew that she was an odd child. Comments like "Do people *dress* like that?" as Danziger left the house haunted her for years.[4] She incorporated this theme into *The Pistachio Prescription*. Cassie feels ugly and worthless and like a plain nobody. She acts out by overindulging in pistachios and plucking her eyebrows. As drastic as these actions seem, Danziger's book is not all serious and depressing. Her witty humor makes the situations feel real, and the characters come alive.

The conflict between Cassie and her mother is clear from the beginning. "Dressed in record time. I can relax for a few minutes. Going back to bed would be great, but I've already made it, and my mother would yell if she saw me on it. I don't see any reason to make a bed since I'm only going to mess it up again at night. Anyway, she's the one who wanted the canopied bed with all the frilly junk that goes with it. I wanted the bed that's shaped like a giant sneaker."[5] Cassie feels misunderstood. She and her mother do not see things in the same way. Her mother is not interested in what will make Cassie truly happy, and this causes conflict.

Even as an adult, Danziger felt like her writing and accomplishments were inadequate for her mother. When Danziger won an award and had to go to Hawaii to receive it, her mother's comment was, "I'll pray that the plane doesn't go down."

With all the negativity from her childhood, Danziger had a lot to overcome. Although she tried to do this in therapy, much of her therapy came from writing. She admitted that *The Pistachio Prescription* was one of the hardest books she had to write. Not only was she dealing with past issues with her mother, but she also had the added pressure of writing yet another great book.

With all the negativity from her childhood, Danziger had a lot to overcome.

"No one told me about 'second-book block.' I was brought up to be a failure, told I was not going to amount to anything."[6] It took Danziger three years to write this book. Of course, Danziger's own doubts about being a good writer only added to her anxiety. Will this book be successful? Will kids like it? What if I'm not as good as people think? These were some of the questions and fears Danziger had. To narrow down what this book is about is difficult. It covers many issues. Danziger said that it is a book about families that cannot make it as a unit, hypochondria, addiction to pistachio nuts, and being able to accept yourself as a winner.[7] Still, she wrote the book, dealt with issues, and touched the hearts of teens. *The*

Pistachio Prescription was a hit, and teens all over the world bought it with great anticipation.

One special moment Danziger would never forget was when a woman asked her to sign a copy of her book *The Pistachio Prescription*. It was for her daughter, Cassie. Danziger thought that it was a coincidence the woman's daughter was named Cassie, too, like the main character. It was no coincidence. The woman told her she named her daughter after the character Cassie. "It means a lot to me, especially since the book was so hard to write, that so many people love and identify with it."[8]

One of Danziger's favorite books to write was *Can You Sue Your Parents for Malpractice?* Apparently, when she was growing up, she threatened her parents by telling them that she would sue them. Instead, she used the threat in the title of this book. It became notorious and some parents did not want their teens to read it, fearing it might put "ideas" in their heads. In spite of this, *Can You Sue Your Parents for Malpractice?* became one of Danziger's most famous books.[9]

It is also considered a sequel to *Cat* although the main character, Lauren Allen, is fourteen years old and has a bit more confidence than Marcy. Her family situation, however, stinks, and Lauren thinks that life is very unfair. "It's absolutely disgusting being fourteen. You've got no rights whatsoever. Your parents get to make all the decisions: Who gets the single bedroom? How much allowance is enough? What time you must come in. Who is a proper friend?"[10]

To make matters worse, Lauren's boyfriend dumps her for a girl whose motto is "Lust Is a Must!" Life is caving in on Lauren, and suing her parents seems like a good idea. When a course is offered at her high school, Law for Children and Young People, Lauren signs up. But Lauren is not serious about suing her parents. And what you might think is another book about a dysfunctional family actually turns into a romantic story about Lauren and the new boy in school, Zack.

What is interesting about this book is that it does not come with a happy ending. Lauren realizes her life is not going to change much, despite what she has learned. She will never change her father, and this is something that Danziger had to also come to terms with. "There's no pretty little package to wrap up. In reality, some people don't change. This book doesn't end happily ever after, and I think that's one of the things kids respond to—it doesn't lie. It's not unhopeful, because Lauren is a real survivor—it's not saying the world is a terrible place. The message is that it ain't always good—you have to work at it, and you may get damaged."[11]

When Danziger was writing this book, she was also teaching eighth and ninth grades. She said she realized it was difficult to be a good teacher. It was also difficult being a good writer. She loved doing both but had to choose one or the other. She chose to write. *Can You Sue Your*

Parents For Malpractice? is dedicated to the students she taught her last year of teaching. This book marks an important transition in her life. Danziger became a full-time writer.

The subjects Danziger wrote about, the titles of her books, and the portrayal of fathers have been frowned upon by some people. Danziger made it clear that she never writes for adults and that staying politically correct just is not honest writing. "If your priority is to offend as few people as possible, you're doing a disservice to your readers, not to mention to yourself as a writer."[12] Most successful writers do not write a book to sell it. They write a book from the heart that will affect their readers and get them to think. Danziger writes to tell the truth, even if the truth hurts.

As Danziger worked out her own problems with her parents and herself, the characters in her books changed too. Divorce was not a subject Danziger was familiar with personally. She never married and her parents never divorced. She did have friends who were divorced, dated divorced men, and taught children who came from divorced homes.

An idea came about when Danziger was taking a class called Writing for Television. One of the assignments was to develop a pilot for a series. Danziger thought that a show about divorce and shared custody would be a good idea, but not for television. A book would be better.

The title came when one day a friend of

Danziger's told her "I just put my kid on the Divorce Express!" Not only was it a great title, but also Danziger's friend and her daughter advised Danziger while writing this book.[13]

When Danziger was growing up, divorce was not nearly as common as it is today. Even in 1984, when *Divorce Express* was published, divorce rates were on a steady climb. The sequel to this book, *It's An Aardvark-Eat-Turtle World* continued the subject of divorce. This is the underlying theme of both books, but to Danziger, "it's not about divorce, it's about living."[14]

Paula Danziger knew she was going to write the sequel to *Divorce Express* while writing it because she genuinely cared about the characters.[15] Phoebe Brook's parents are divorced and she finds

> ## "If you take the letters in the word DIVORCES, and rearrange them, they spell DISCOVER."

herself in the middle. She is shuffled around from one parent's home to another, having two homes, two lifestyles, two sets of friends, two sets of clothing. Sometimes it is too much for Phoebe to take, and *Divorce Express* deals with her situation. *Divorce Express* is one of the first books written for teens that not only discusses this subject in detail, but also shows how kids are adversely affected by divorce. But it also shows something else. It shows a main character who is made stronger by learning to cope with the problems in her family. Phoebe says, "I've learned something else too. If you take the letters in the word DIVORCES, and rearrange them, they spell DISCOVER."[16]

The unusual title, *It's An Aardvark-Eat-Turtle World*, is created by the main character, Rosie. Her father is always saying, "it's a dog-eat-dog world." Rosie puts a twist on this and instead says, "It's an aardvark-eat-turtle world."[17] As usual, it is classic Danziger. This book has a new main character because Danziger felt that Phoebe from *Divorce Express* was too angry at the end of the book and too "new" in coping with divorce. Danziger wanted a character who had lived with the situation for years. Rosie was the obvious choice.

This book also handles another issue not much talked about in children's literature. When Rosie's mother marries Phoebe's dad in *Divorce Express*, we find out that Rosie is from interracial parents. Her mother is white and her father is African American. The *Interracial Books for Children Bulletin* recommended the book as the first they had seen that "approaches the subject of interracial children and some of the problems they encounter."[18]

Danziger felt that there were too few books with interracial families or African-American children on the covers. She worried about being politically correct, too, but soon realized that she was just writing about people and their experiences. She was writing about kids trying to get through life.[19]

Danziger seemed to write on the cutting edge. She did not start writing a book thinking that the subject would be popular in a few years. She wrote about what she saw and experienced, whether it was in her own life or her friends' or students' lives. Danziger's books are as relevant today as they were twenty years ago because the issues that affect teens have not changed much. When a writer is honest about the issues, the writing becomes timeless. This was true for Danziger. "All writers write from deep experience. For me, that is childhood. From it flow feelings of vulnerability, compassion, and strength. Perhaps it would be better to say that I write 'of' young people rather than 'for' or 'to' them."[20]

Chapter 5

Outer Space, New York, and London

"I spend a lot of time in London, England. I love it there and I can speak the language!"[1]

Danziger rocketed into another world when she wrote *This Place Has No Atmosphere*. Some fans wondered why she would write a story that took place in the year 2057 and on another planet, but for Danziger it was simple. "I love science fiction and I especially liked Asimov and Bradbury as a kid—*Illustrated Man, Dangerous Visions*. My strength is not plot, but I thought I'd try it."[2]

Again, Danziger writes about a timeless and relevant theme. Families move more today than ever before. Still, this book, written for kids in middle schools, will find a likable main character who has a difficult time adjusting to a new place. Aurora is devastated. She does not want to move to a colony on the moon and leave her boyfriend and the school where she feels important.[3] Staying positive is hard, especially when she feels the colony has "no atmosphere."

Aurora soon learns to adjust and discovers some things about herself. She likes little kids and realizes that she is not the center of the universe. For Danziger, this realization came later in life. "When you're that angry, it takes longer."[4] It is a hard lesson for all teens to come to terms with, and some do not. Danziger felt this was an important issue to tackle in her story. Other issues are relevant too, such as drug use and the holistic medicine, which Danziger, herself, used to help with pain.

Danziger strongly believed in the use of holistic medicine and the healing power of hands. "As people we all have a quality inside ourselves that we can center and calm enough to help others. For someone whose hands go out of sockets, I have discovered an incredible strength and gentleness in my hands."[5] Danziger, herself, used acupuncture for many years.

Danziger has a keen ear for teenage jokes and chatter; puns, some witty and some corny, punctuate the realistic dialogue. Aurora's story suggests to middle school readers that the teens of 2057 will suffer the same bittersweet emotions as those of today, and that caring friends, a loving family, and a sense of humor are important anywhere, anytime.[6] "Some things don't change." Danziger asserted. "Parents are still going to fight with kids in a hundred years."[7] Aurora's relationship with her own mother is difficult. Her mother can read minds and, what is worse, she can read Aurora's.

What could be more fun than a scavenger hunt around New York City? To Kendra, a lot. She is the main character in Danziger's next book, *Remember Me to Harold Square*. The last thing this fifteen year old wants to do is spend the summer searching for clues with her family.

Danziger loved big cities. Living in New York City was exciting. She loved going to the theater and shopping. One of her favorite expressions was "Charge it!"[8]

Kendra is unlike the other heroines in Danziger's books. She is more mature and not angry. Instead, Kendra is seeking enlightenment. Danziger uses a metaphor throughout the story relating butterflies to the changes in a young girl's body. "Just as soon as you get used to things being one way, you turn into something else—a butterfly or what books refer to as 'a young adult.'"[9]

Danziger uses the scavenger hunt in two ways. She shows how Kendra grows and matures, and she touts New York City. Danziger brings the city to life in a way teens can relate to.[10]

Danziger's popularity spread worldwide. She began dividing her time between New York and London. Danziger had a special fondness for London and its people. They took to her as well.

While Carrie, Danziger's only niece, was growing up she spent a lot of time with Danziger and

even traveled with her to England. Paula was
Carrie's best friend.

> "I read Paula's novels, even though I used to tell her
> that I didn't. . . . I don't know why I told her that, I
> think it was just to torture her. I was always a sci-
> ence and animal person and Paula was always very
> much books and jewelry and we used to have fun
> torturing each other. Paula's books did not particu-
> larly impact me, at least not in comparison. Paula
> herself impacted me in every way possible, but not
> so much through her writing but by just being the
> amazing person that she was. On the issue of talking
> to Paula about teen problem[s] . . . Paula was my
> best friend, I told her everything and we discussed it
> all!"[11]

Carrie was the initial inspiration for the Amber
Brown character. Writing for girls ages eight to
twelve was new, since most of Danziger's books
were focused on teens. She originally only planned
to write one Amber Brown book, but the character
was so beloved, the series grew to fifteen books.
Carrie originally gave Danziger two plots to write
about: her best friend having moved away and a
story about chicken pox in England. Danziger took
these ideas and created the rest of the Amber
Brown stories from the vision in her head.[12]

Danziger was writing the books for the
Matthew Martin series, based on her nephews,
and Carrie constantly asked her to write a book for
the same age group for girls. It would be a few
years later when Danziger's first Amber Brown
book was published in 1994. It was titled, *Amber
Brown Is Not a Crayon*.

The origin of Amber Brown's name, however, is

a joke between fellow writers. When author and illustrators Marc and Laurie Brown—the creators of a multitude of best-selling books about Arthur the Aardvark and his sister D.W.—were expecting a child, Danziger suggested that they name their baby Amber.[13]

"Then everyone would call her Crayola Face," Danziger told them. Instead, the Browns named their daughter Eliza, and now she receives advance copies of the Amber Brown books for critique.[14]

> # Carrie Danziger was the initial inspiration for the Amber Brown character.

Much of what happened in Carrie's life happened in the Amber Brown books too. Carrie's best friends moved at one point, and she really did get the chicken pox in England, which happened in the second Amber Brown book, *You Can't Eat Your Chicken Pox, Amber Brown*. Danziger originally envisioned her story in picture book form, but during the revision process discovered that it needed an older voice. As a result, the novels are chapter books for beginning readers, an audience often neglected in the publishing world.[15]

Carrie seemed to like the idea that one of Danziger's characters was based on her. She helped Danziger proof the books but made it very clear that writing was not her "thing":

> When Amber was still a pattern of ideas and thoughts in Paula's head, Paula would tell me what was going on with Amber and where she wanted the story to go. She did, however, take into consideration my thoughts. For example, I was the one who pointed out that as Amber got older, she probably shouldn't wear pigtails anymore. I might have had a few ideas, but writing was always Paula's thing, and she was so good at it. I didn't actually read a lot of the Amber books until they were in proof. Paula would have them sitting on a shelf in her Manhattan apartment and I would pick them up and just start reading them.[16]

In the 1990s she was a popular contributor on the children's Saturday morning show, *Going Live*. Here, Danziger encouraged children to read by interviewing other well-known authors and giving book reviews. The name *Going Live* was later changed to *Live and Kicking*.

"Most writers are invisible and can walk easily through the streets," she said. "I still get stopped a lot in England because of TV."[17]

One author interviewed for the show was Dick King-Smith, who wrote the book *The Sheep-Pig*, published in Britain. This book became better known as the movie *Babe*. A city girl at heart, Danziger was not well suited for the interview in the English countryside. She was inappropriately dressed right down to her footwear and claimed to be allergic to everything she came in contact with.[18] Carrie never saw a taping of the show, but she did visit the BBC building once where

Paula Danziger enjoys a ride on a Good Humor
ice cream truck.

Danziger worked. There was one room in
particular that Carrie remembered well. The room
was where Danziger chose the books she would
review for the show. Carrie also recalled a closet.
It was the prize vault. It held toys and prizes that
were given out on the show to children. The cast
loved it when Danziger arrived because she would
bring American candy like Nerds and Bubble Tape.
They were not available in England in the early
1990s. Danziger stashed the candy along with
other fun prizes in the closet.[19]

"I remember once, Paula was telling me, that
she brought Bubble Tape over to give out as
prizes," Carrie recalled. "And they announced a

winner for the Bubble Tape, but the host, Phillip, had eaten half of it, thinking that Paula had brought it over for him. So she ended up having to send more Bubble Tape over to give to the girl as a prize. Phillip really loved Bubble Tape."[20]

Danziger's relationship with her niece was special. "When I got older was when I really got to know the going-ons of Paula's life and it became a real friendship between the two of us. It was no longer a love just between two family members, it became the whole package. It was the time when we really became best friends."[21]

Danziger's family was very important to her. She dedicated her book *Remember Me to Harold Square* to the Danzigers: Barry, Annette, Sam'l, Carrie, and "Mr. Ben" Danziger.

Chapter 6

Books for Boys

In the late 1980s and early 1990s, Danziger did something she had never done before. She published books for boys. In 1989, she published *Everyone Else's Parents Said Yes*; in 1990, *Make Like a Tree and Leave*; in 1991, *Earth to Matthew*; and in 1992, *Not for a Billion Gazillion Dollars*. These books featured the adorably naughty character, Matthew Martin.

All of Danziger's previous books had teen girls as the main character, often with pesky little brothers. Writing a book from a boy's point of view was a real change for Danziger, and she loved doing it.

Matthew Martin, the protagonist in the "Matthew Martin" series of books, is based on her nephews, but especially on Sam Danziger and the time Paula Danziger spent with him. He was nine when her first book, *Everyone Else's Parents Said Yes*, came out.

"Paula did indeed use me as 'inspiration' for Matthew Martin. However how much he was based on me is pretty questionable," said Sam Danziger. Even Danziger acknowledged that Martin was partly based on Sam and her two other nephews. Matthew, like all her characters, was a composite.[1]

"I remember when I first saw the cover I said to Paula something like, 'This book is supposed to be about me, but the picture on the cover looks a lot more like my friend Todd.' And I remember the problems that Matthew faced were very different from the sort of things that I faced."[2]

Sam acknowledged that while he was perhaps the seed for Matthew, the town of Califon, New Jersey, and the middle school were even bigger influences. Danziger's brother and his family lived in Califon and so she knew a lot about the town and area. One teacher in Danziger's book might have been based on a beloved teacher in Califon, New Jersey, according to Sam. Mrs. Stanton, the teacher in *Everyone Else's Parents Said Yes*, is strict, fair, and kind to the children and seems to understand Matthew. When Matthew creates a mean greeting card for his sister, calling her four-eyes, Mrs. Stanton intervenes. After all, it is supposed to be a nice card.

> "It's your choice, Matthew. Throw the card away now and be able to use the computer later for your

invitations, or hold on to the card and not be able to use the computer later for your invitations."

"Aw." Matthew knows he has been beaten. "I'll throw the card out now."

"Good boy," Mrs. Stanton says."

It was not unusual for Danziger to visit classrooms around the country. This way she met the children and the teachers who might one day be an inspiration for her books. Sam noted, "Paula would frequently come to Califon to give book

Paula Danziger with her sister-in-law, Annette; nephews Sam and Josh; and niece Carrie.

talks usually to [our] class. . . . As per typical
Paula, she spent lots of time talking with the children, and thus got a general idea of what a ten
year old at Califon was like, rather than myself
per-se."[4]

Sam felt his biggest contribution to the
Matthew Martin books came when he helped
Danziger as she wrote sequels. Danziger would
read the stories to Sam. He would question things
Matthew said or how he thought and felt.

> Maybe the biggest direct contribution occurred when
> she was reading one of the sequels to me. She wrote
> something like, "Matthew belched the . . . " and I
> asked her, "What does belched mean?"
>
> She answered, "It means burped. Do you think
> that's a word sixth graders wouldn't know?"
>
> So I answered, "No, leave it in, now that you've
> told me what it means, it's fine."[5]

At the time Danziger began writing the
Matthew Martin books, she was also just starting
to use a computer. She had a lot of problems learning the computer and would call either Sam or her
brother, Barry, for help. Barry said that this time
was special because it opened up a lot of commu-
nication between them. Paula was not computer
savvy. Once she called Barry because her computer screen would not come on.

"Did you try pushing the ON button, Paula?"
"Oh, it works!" said Paula.[6]

Not only did Danziger write from a different
perspective, that of a boy, but she also wrote her
stories targeting a different age group. The
Matthew Martin books really were targeted for

boys ages nine to twelve, although struggling teens might still appreciate the antics of Matthew Martin and the easier to read language. Books for boys were in need, and Danziger filled that niche with Matthew. She found an entirely new group of readers who would come to love her stories—boys.

Matthew Martin seems to be a typical boy in *Everyone Else's Parents Said Yes*. Danziger's experience in teaching and working with middle school and high school students allowed her to clearly grasp the difficulties kids have growing up.

Things are going well for Matthew Martin in the beginning of the story. His birthday is coming up, and making plans for it has never been more fun. But then, life happens. Matthew's best friends get mad at him, and the girls at school, annoyed with Matthew's pranks, decide to get even. Why is everything going wrong for Matthew? It is not his fault, or is it? Matthew can not seem to stop the pestering, whether it is the girls at school or his sister, Amanda.

> Amanda does not quit. "And it's not fair. Look at that little twerp. He doesn't have to wear glasses."
>
> "That's because they like me better than they like you," Matthew teases. "And my ears aren't even lopsided."
>
> Matthew has trouble stopping once he starts. "And I'm not ugly, and dumb, and acting like a turkey."
>
> Amanda stands up. "You repulsive little runt."
>
> Matthew goes to his room and thinks about what he's done. Nothing.
>
> It is Amanda's fault.
>
> It always is.

> Someday he thinks, *someday*, I'm going to get even.[7]

Danziger did not marry nor have children of her own, so she often "adopted" other writer's children. She listened to kids and read their letters. Danziger used a lot of what they suggested or shared in her stories. She even dedicated her book *Everyone Else's Parents Said Yes* to "The Kids All Over the Country Who Have Shared Their Ideas, Experiences, and Suggestions."[8]

Children were important to Danziger. She especially loved her nephews and niece and often took them on trips to different parts of the country and the world.

"Paula thought that it was very important for us to travel. She always firmly believed that there was a whole world out there that we weren't experiencing living in small-town New Jersey and we should go see it," said Sam Danziger.[9]

While with them, Danziger not only got to spend quality time with her family, but she also got to see firsthand how children acted, reacted, and interacted with her and the people around her. Danziger and her nephews and niece shared many fun and interesting experiences while traveling. And sometimes Danziger would incorporate these experiences into her books.

One such visit occurred in her book *Earth to Matthew*. In one of the last of the series of Matthew Martin books, Danziger has created a more mature Matthew. He is growing up and it shows in the way he treats people. He finds himself liking one particular girl named Jill. When she talks to him, he feels funny inside and this causes confusion. Boys are not supposed to like girls—or are they? Having worked with preteens, Danziger understood the complexities, the problems kids at this age deal with, and wrote about it in an honest manner. Matthew is changing in many ways, and he wants to be taken more seriously at school and at home.

> ## Danziger understood the complexities, the problems kids at this age deal with.

Matthew's class is working hard on a project about ecosystems. Danziger weaves in lots of teen-appropriate environmental facts as well as plenty of jokes about diapers and toilets.[10] The reward at the end of the book is a trip to the Franklin Institute in Philadelphia, Pennsylvania. It is an overnight trip just like the one Danziger made with her nephew Sam. This was a special trip for both of them.

"For me the coolest part of the whole Matthew Martin series was the trip to the Franklin Institute of Technology (in Philadelphia). Aunt took me on the overnight camping trip and that was really great. I even still have the red bag that appeared on the cover of the book."[11]

For Danziger, writing the Matthew books was a

joy. "I really love Matthew," she wrote at the same time she was working on the last book, *Not for a Billion Gazillion Dollars*. What Danziger liked best was that Matthew grew and changed. He developed a social conscience while still maintaining a high sense of play. "A high sense of play is something I value in myself, so I really like Matthew."[12]

While some memories were fun, others were not. Sam related this event: "When I was fourteen or so, my aunt and I had a really disastrous trip to Toronto. The high point was when I found a fingernail in my hamburger at the revolving restaurant!"

Danziger always had an itinerary when she traveled. It was not so much the places they went and the things they saw that mattered. It was the people they met. Danziger was a people person. But according to Sam, who preferred to break into a sweat and see all that he could see, Danziger had a difficult time getting around. So walking to sights and events was hard.

"The last trip we were together on was up to San Francisco. Paula spent a lot of time in the hotel while my brother Josh and I [Sam] went out and explored the city. Speaking very frankly, a lot of this was because Paula was [overweight], and ultimately, this killed her (both the heart disease and the complications thereafter)."[13]

Danziger made the best of her trips. She may not have been able to keep up with her young nephews the way she would have liked, but she did make it fun. Sam recalled a game they played one night in a restaurant during their trip to San Francisco. The game was called "Who do you want on your island?"

> It started with a question like, "If you could have three people, living or dead, alive on your island, who would they be?" And led to questions, "If you could have one president, or three world leaders, or two movie stars, etc." Paula's island was a large full-service hotel populated by people like JFK (there not for his politics, but "just for fun"), where everything just happened and worked for you. Paula told me that she would really like to visit my island, but needed to get into good enough shape to be able to climb the mountain."[14]

Danziger's imagination and playfulness helped her to create, and she loved it. So did her family. She incorporated this into her character, Matthew Martin. It worked well and boys loved reading about Matthew because they understood what it was like to be an eleven-year-old boy. Apparently, so did Danziger.

Chapter 7

Collaboration

When the idea to collaborate on a story with another author was brought up to Danziger, she hesitated. She had tried this before and it did not work out. Free spirit that she was, Danziger enjoyed working on her own, in her own style, space, and time. When she met with Ann M. Martin, a seasoned writer who had written the series *The Baby-sitters Club*, as well as many other books, Paula knew that this could work. However, the meeting of two great writing minds did not come without its share of problems.

Both Paula Danziger and Ann Martin had concerns. "I like writing from outlines; Paula didn't believe in them. I like deadlines; Paula hated them. I like proper punctuation; Paula thought that it was fine to put 20 dots in an ellipsis."[1]

The differences between the two were remarkable. Two people could not be more different. But to Danziger, "in ways that matter most" they were compatible: they have good senses of humor, are deeply compassionate.[2] Martin loves animals, and Danziger was allergic to them. Danziger hated sewing, while Martin loves to sew. Danziger loved to speak in public. Martin hates it. Danziger loved to shop, but Martin would watch her spending, and buy little at times.[3] Even at their first meeting at Scholastic, it was clear to everyone which author would assume which character. Danziger arrived wearing glitter, a sparkly scarf, and a sweeping dress. Ann wore corduroy pants and, as Danziger noted, a shirt that looked like something the *Where's Waldo* guy would wear.[4]

It is no wonder that the two authors brought themselves a bit into the characters of Elizabeth and Tara*Starr. According to Ann Martin, Elizabeth is quiet and shy. "Elizabeth tends to be a little more conservative in her dress, to like to spend time alone, and yet she has a wonderful relationship with this—this friend who is so different and so outgoing."[5]

Danziger's Tara*Starr is the opposite. "She doesn't always think before she speaks. She's very opinionated, and has a great—a great flair about her, is—is not the kind of person who likes to be alone in a room as much. She likes to be out there meeting new people, doing new things, trying new things out."[6]

The difference in personalities worked, and in 1996, Danziger and Martin began writing their first novel together. It was called, *P.S. Longer Letter Later*. The two were initially brought together by a fan who thought the writers should know one another. They met over dinner and discovered they were compatible in many ways. According to Ann Martin, both she and Danziger had a similar sense of humor and were devoted to their work.[7] The two writers became good friends. At the time, Holt editor Laura Goodwin, who was also a friend of both writers, suggested that they co-produce a novel constructed of letters.[8]

P.S. Longer Letter Later destroyed the myth that writing has to be a solitary pursuit, according to editors Brenda Bowen and Craig Walker at Scholastic.[9] "The collaboration is sure to please both halves of the female middle-school population: those who relish the type of hilarity found in Danziger's books, and those who prefer the quieter, more measured style of Martin's writing."[10] Each writer took on a character. Danziger is the glitz-loving Tara*Starr, and her best friend, Elizabeth, is written by Ann Martin. Although the characters are not biographical, they reflect the diverse personalities found in each writer.

Apparently, opposites do attract. Danziger and Martin were good examples of that and so were their characters, Tara*Starr and Elizabeth. Both came from very different backgrounds. The two eleven-year-old girls have different personalities. But when Tara*Starr moves away, the two best friends become pen pals. They realize that their friendship has changed and try to cope. From the very first page, the reader sees how difficult this is. In a society where families often move, it is easy to see why *P.S. Longer Letter Later* became an important book for middle schoolers and young teens.

Often it is easier to communicate via letter. Sharing emotions, especially for young girls, can be easier when done in writing. The correspondence between Tara*Starr and Elizabeth feels real.

Page one, as with many of Danziger's and Martin's books, opens with drama. Elizabeth is writing to Tara*Starr who has moved. This is her first letter to her best friend.

> September 4
>
> Dear Tara*Starr,
>
> It's 4:02 p.m. and I'm sitting in my room at the end of the first day of seventh grade, and I can't help what I am going to say next.
>
> I AM SO MAD AT YOU. WHY DID YOU HAVE TO MOVE AWAY??? I THOUGHT WE WERE SUP-POSED TO BE BEST FRIENDS 4-EVER. IF I DIDN'T LIKE YOU SO MUCH I WOULD HAVE MADE YOU MY EX-BEST FRIEND 4-EVER BY NOW.
>
> Okay. There. I just had to say that.[11]

When the story first began, Danziger noted that she and Ann Martin discussed the backgrounds of the characters and then began faxing letters back and forth in the voices of Tara*Starr and Elizabeth.[12] Much of the story was worked out as

Paula Danziger and Ann Martin (left).

they wrote letters back and forth. The two writers knew that while Tara*Starr's family grew up, came together, and became more stable, Elizabeth's would fall apart. But the plot and conflicts were worked out as the letters continued.

Danziger felt that the plot was the hardest part to write when it came to *P.S. Longer Letter Later*.[13] Often their letters were discussions about how to handle different situations.

Plot was often difficult for Danziger. She could develop great characters but often there were no plots in her stories. When Bruce Coville would read her stories before they went to the publisher, he would ask Danziger, "What's the plot?"[14] It seemed to be a chronic problem in Danziger's books, but she was always able to work it out, giving each story a solid plot.

Even though Danziger never liked didactic books—stories that taught a lesson or conveyed a strong message—her books were filled with them. In *P.S. Longer Letter Later*, Danziger's message is clear: "No matter how different people can be, if you care about each other, and you're friends, and you grow and learn and accept the person who is, not what you want that person to be, there's a chance to really be friends forever."[15]

Acceptance is an ongoing theme in Danziger's books, whether it is being accepted by a parent, a friend, or people in general. For Danziger, it was important that people loved her for who she was and not for whom they wanted her to be.

P.S. Longer Letter Later got rave reviews. "[A] spirited and readable book with none of the anemia or tendentiousness that weighs down some writing for young people," wrote *The New York Times Book Review*.[16]

The sequel to *P.S. Longer Letter Later* was *Snail Mail No More*. The long-distance friendship and all its drama continues between Elizabeth and Tara*Starr, only now, technology has caught up. The girls are able to e-mail each other. The girls have not changed much since the first book, but major life events threaten their friendship.

Danziger looked at both of the books as one book. She enjoyed writing them, but *Snail Mail No More* was really a continuation of *P.S. Longer Letter*

Later. Martin enjoyed writing the second book more than the first.[17]

The ending is poignant as the two girls resolve the many problems throughout the book. But perhaps the ending says a lot about Danziger, the author behind Tara*Starr who wrote this passage:

> Thinking about life as a book is really great. . . . You know what I like best!?! We'll always be characters in each other's 'books' . . . and even when there are 'bad' things written on our 'pages,' we'll always be there, as real people, to help each other out.
>
> Have I told you lately that I'm glad we are friends?
>
> Love,
> Tara*[18]

Perhaps Danziger saw her own life as a book. It was a story with many ups and downs, conflicts to resolve, and friendships to be made. Danziger's life was all about writing. She took those experiences and incorporated them into her books. When she had the idea for *United Tates of America*, published in 2002, her original plan was to write fifty books, one for each state. Since she loved to travel and meet new people, this idea seemed perfect. Danziger decided to write one book a month, but the thought overwhelmed her.[19]

The idea was put on hold, and Danziger visited friends in Pennsylvania. This is where she became involved in scrapbooking. She loved art, and, although she never was recognized for her artistic abilities, she enjoyed colors and shapes and putting them together. Scrapbooking seemed odd to Danziger, who had never really kept photos

Paula Danziger plays the part of one of Santa's helpers during the Christmas holiday.

or mementos of her life or career. She did not have children or pets, yet the idea intrigued her.

Danziger was invited to a "cropping" party. Here she saw people cutting up photos and artistically placing them in scrapbooks with stickers, blocks of color, and shapes and then penning in information about the people and places in the photos. But there was something deeper to scrapbooking that interested Danziger. "Here were people keeping track of their lives and their family's lives; scout meetings, school events, family occasions, lots of things I write about, but don't get involved with too often."[20]

But this one day led to a three-day weekend event of scrapbooking. This event changed how Danziger looked at scrapbooking as well as her own life. But Danziger was not going to scrapbook her own life. Instead, she used the experience to help create a character in her book. Danziger was struggling with the main character, Skate Tate. It seemed strange that Danziger would struggle to create a character since her previous protagonists were always so diverse and interesting. Through her scrapbooking experience, she created a character who would use her creative abilities to document both the simple and extraordinary events in her life.[21] Danziger had a good friend who also enjoyed scrapbooking. Danziger used her family and their scrapbooks as the basis of her book *United Tates of America*.

While she was working on this book, Danziger had an experience she would never forget. It happened while she was traveling in Reno, Nevada. Someone tried to rob Danziger. She was badly beaten. She experienced post-traumatic stress syndrome, and found it difficult to function in everyday life. That meant not traveling. Danziger stayed home. "I kept organizing and reorganizing my apartment. I bought a labeler and labeled practically everything in my storage areas. It was obvious to me I wanted order in my life and no surprises."[22]

Danziger continued to write *United Tates of America* and used her own feelings in the book. Skate Tate does not like change, and this is an issue she deals with in her book. She also wanted Skate's uncle to be a memorable character so that when he dies, the reader can connect with Skate as she goes through the grieving process. This book deals with many issues, including loss, sadness, grief, loneliness, and guilt. But Danziger is quick to add, "It's a book about hope and care. Sad as well as funny, it's a book about life."[23]

United Tates of America was the last novel Danziger would write for teens.

Chapter 8

Danziger's Legacy

When Danziger suddenly fell ill in June of 2004, her friends and family came to be by her side. Everyone fully expected her to make a recovery and get back to writing, including Danziger, herself. She was in good spirits. But a lifetime of battling obesity got the best of her. Her nephew Sam Danziger said that her heart just could not sustain her body.

Early June 2004 Paula Danziger was at her apartment in New York City. Her niece, Carrie, was visiting. Paula was not doing well. She kept thinking she had acid reflux and took the medications doctors had prescribed for it. But by seven the next morning, Carrie was deeply concerned. Danziger woke Carrie up, telling her she did not feel well. Danziger did not look well. She took some more medication, and Carrie stayed in bed with her. But the pain kept getting worse. Danziger told Carrie that her arm hurt, too, because she had fallen asleep with her bra on and that she had heartburn. Carrie knew something was not right. She got some neighbors to come over. One of the neighbors had experienced a heart attack before and knew right away that Danziger was probably having one too. While they sat with Danziger, Carrie called 911. She heard Danziger say, "I think I'm having a heart attack, but don't tell Carrie. I don't want to ruin her day." They immediately called an ambulance and rushed Danziger to the hospital. "That crazy woman loved me so much that she was putting me above herself," said Carrie.[1]

Danziger actually had her heart attack in the hospital. The doctors ran tests to determine the blockage in her arteries. The damage was severe. They worked on Danziger to keep her alive. She fought for a month.[2] "I swore that Paula was going to make it through," said Carrie. "She was a fighter from the beginning, right up to the end."[3]

Sam Danziger recalled that his aunt was never fully cognizant after that heart attack. Danziger suffered cardiac cell death. She also had ARDS, acute respiratory distress syndrome and organ stress. Danziger died of complications due to a heart attack on July 8, 2004, at age fifty-nine. Her brother Barry reflected:

> Paula was my sister (and will always remain as such) for 59 years. We did not get along for over 20 years. Sometime, around the 21st year, a bond started to

form. It grew when I got married and had kids she could adopt. During the last 30 years, we got very close—and REALIZED ALL THE TIME WE MISSED, and all the wasted effort expended in feeling ill of each other. I will miss not being able to call her and finding out "what's happenin." I will miss goofing on each other at a seconds notice. I will miss that period of time when we did not get along. But what I will miss most of that period is the wasted time we spent not getting along, goofing, showing that we loved each other.[4]

When Paula Danziger passed away, it affected many people. Friends could not believe that Danziger was gone. It was sudden and she was much too young, yet she lives on in her books and characters like Marcy Lewis and Amber Brown. Generations of teens will continue to read her books.

"In real life, as in books, she had the gift for creating intimacy, friends who could share their deepest fears, loves, and hopes as well as laughs," said Elizabeth Levy, close friend. Danziger and she both published with Dell in the 1970s. They would meet up at conventions, but then go their own ways until one day Danziger called her up and gave her an ultimatum. Danziger told Levy, "We've got to put up or shut up. We're either good friends or not." They became good friends.[5]

Bruce Coville was another favorite friend of Danziger's. He first met Danziger at a librarian's conference in South Carolina. They were both accepting a Children's Choice award. Bruce chuckled as he told this story. Once they were both seated at the table, Danziger got up.

"Where are you going?" he asked.

"Watch," she said. Danziger stood up and proceeded to navigate around the room talking to everyone she could. She was not shy. She introduced herself and got to know some of the people in the room.

"It was a brilliant idea," said Bruce. "Everyone in the room loved her before she got up to speak."[6]

Danziger knew how to work an audience, and to speak in front of people, but it was more than

Paula Danziger continues to serve as an inspiration to family, friends, colleagues, and fans.

this. According to Bruce Coville, it was her generosity of spirit, and her love for people that made her such a memorable person.

Their friendship grew and Danziger and Bruce Coville would help each other with their stories over the phone. They worked at refining their stories and teaching each other about writing in the process. "It is not often that someone can be simultaneously a great teacher and a great friend. Paula was both of those, to her it came naturally."[7]

Doug Whiteman, executive vice president of Penguin Group, Inc., and president of Penguin Young Readers Group, said, "We have lost not only an extraordinary writer, but also an extremely caring, giving person. Paula will long be remembered for the many hours she gave to aspiring writers and young editors as she tried to help bring along the next generation of publishing talent. All of us at Penguin loved her dearly and will miss her humor, warmth, and compassion."[8]

Author Pamela Curtis Swallow remembers the night Danziger passed away. "The evening was ablaze—like a giant Fourth of July sparkler shooting red, orange, gold, and purple glitter skyward and off the facades of the building. A fitting tribute and dazzling sendoff to a life that was over too soon."[9] The sunset sky was indicative of Paula—colorful and dazzling.

Colleagues could not imagine a conference without Paula Danziger. She lit up the room and made people laugh; she made them feel good about themselves.

People who knew her for only a moment also felt a great loss. She inspired so many people to achieve their dreams and goals to write for children. "We've been robbed of a great gift," said one writer. "Paula was an early influence on my career," says another.

One writer remembers a time when a young student was in a horrible car crash and in a coma. Danziger sent her letters and called her on the phone. She sent her books and helped the girl in her recovery.[10]

Shortly before Danziger was hospitalized, she, her nephew Sam, and her Aunt Fran were out eating at an Italian restaurant. Rather suddenly, Paula took their hands and said, "This is what I love most, bringing people that I love together." Looking back, it certainly seemed like the kind of thing someone would say to build a legacy, a way to be remembered.[11]

Danziger's last book, surprisingly enough, was not a book written for teens or for her Amber Brown series. It was something she had not written before, a picture book. *Barfburger Baby, I Was Here First* is classic Danziger. It is a sweet story about sibling rivalry from the day the new baby arrives home. Suddenly the attention is not on five-year-old Jonathon anymore. Danziger captured both the humor and reality of being an only child and then an older sibling. She never saw the release of her first picture book, but no doubt, she knew it would be a hit.

Danziger's books have sold in the millions. They are beloved around the world and are sold in many different languages, including French and Spanish. Danziger loved to travel and meet the children who read her books. She traveled the country, giving lectures and visiting schools. She also put in extended visits of several days in length at various schools so that she could talk in depth with students.[12]

Danziger's generosity had no boundaries. She not only loved to talk about her books, her writing, and her family, but she also loved to listen to other writers and learn about their books. Some advice she often gave conference attendees was this: Make it special.

That is exactly what Danziger did—everything and everyone she came in contact with she made special.

"Well, in my next life, I want to be tall and thin, [be able to] parallel park and make good coffee. But for now, I have lots of stuff to work out in my life, but I'll have that until the day I die. I want to write more books."[13]

In Her Own Words

The following are quotes from Paula Danziger from a variety of print and Web sources, as well as personal interviews conducted by the author with Ms. Danziger's family.

Paula on Paula

Apparently I was funny as long as anyone could remember.[1]

I loved books—they were a way to get out of my life. If it had print on it, I read it.[2]

I still use that line, "I think I can, I think I can, I know I can" before anything that makes me nervous—a speech or a big date or doing a TV show.[3]

The only other thing I would consider doing now, is being on TV or stand up comedy.[4]

A high sense of play is something that I value in myself.[5]

This is what I love most, bringing people that I love together.[6]

On family

We were just Danzigers.[7]

When my father would yell at me, I'd tell myself, "Someday I'll use this in a book."[8]

We were a nuclear family only in the sense of being explosive.[9]

My mother wanted me to be a nurse, so I thought becoming a speech therapist was like being a nurse without the blood.[10]

On people

[I]t's about living. I write about life. People sometimes go. Fathers sometimes leave. It's not all fun and games.[11]

In reality, some people don't change.[12]

Remember, the most important thing you can create is yourself as wonderful people![13]

On the craft of writing

He [John Ciardi] taught me a lot about language. [He suggested that she analyze one poem by underlining the funny lines in red and the serious lines in blue. By the end of the poem, Ciardi said, you get purple. That's what I always write toward, that mixture.[14]

I wrote what I knew best. I was a fat little teenager from New Jersey who hated school with a younger brother who stuck orange pits in his bear.[15]

All writers write from deep experience. For me, that is childhood. From it flow feelings of vulnerability, compassion, and strength. Perhaps it would be better to say that I write "of" young people rather than "for" or "to" them.[16]

I made the choice long ago to write about real life. And life is both serious and funny.[17]

I love science fiction and I especially liked Asimov and Bradbury as a kid—*Illustrated Man*, *Dangerous Visions*. My strength is not plot, but I thought I'd try it.[18]

I think every writer wants to tell the best story they know how to tell, and let people get what they're going to get from it.[19]

On children

I don't come down to kids' level. I respond on a level I feel comfortable on.[20]

[Going to camp is] a time when kids leave home, meet new people and try out new behavior.[21]

My strength as a teacher was that I really cared about kids, books, and creativity.[22]

Chronology

1944—Paula Danziger is born on August 18 in Washington, D.C.

1947—Brother, Barry, is born.

1955—Family moves to Metuchen, New Jersey.

1963—Attends Montclair State College, New Jersey.

1967—Receives her B.A. in English.

1967–1971—Title 1 teacher in Edison, Highland Park, Newark, and West Orange junior high schools, New Jersey.

1968–1970—Works as English teacher, Lincoln Junior High School, West Orange, New Jersey.

1970—Seriously injured in two car accidents.

1971—Begins writing *The Cat Ate My Gymsuit*.

1972–1978—Counselor, coordinator of tutorial services, and supervisor of reading faculty at Montclair State College.

1973—Receives M.A. in reading, Montclair State College.

1974–1976—Freelance reader for Dell Publishing Company.

1974—Publishes *The Cat Ate My Gymsuit*.

1978—Publishes *The Pistachio Prescription*.

1979—Publishes *Can You Sue Your Parents for Malpractice?* Becomes a full-time writer.

1980—Publishes *There's a Bat in Bunk Five*.

1984—Publishes *The Divorce Express*.

1985—Publishes *It's an Aardvark-Eat-Turtle World*.

1986—Publishes *This Place Has No Atmosphere*.

1987—Publishes *Remember Me to Harold Square*.

1989—Publishes *Everyone Else's Parents Said Yes*.

1990—Publishes *Make Like a Tree and Leave*.

1991—Publishes *Earth to Matthew*. Appears as a regular contributor on BBC-TV in England on *Going Live!*

1992—Publishes *Not for a Billion Gazillion Dollars*.

1994—Publishes *Amber Brown Is Not a Crayon* and *Thames Doesn't Rhyme with James*.

1997—Becomes a member of the Society of Children's Book Writers and Illustrator's advisory board.

1998—Publishes *P.S. Longer Letter Later*, collaboration with Ann Martin.

1999—Publishes *Snail Mail No More*, collaboration with Ann Martin.

2002— Publishes *United Tates of America*.

2004—Dies, July 8, 2004 in New York City, age fifty-nine. Paula's first picture book, *Barfburger Baby, I Was Here First*, is published in September.

Chapter Notes

Chapter 1. Funny Girl

1. Eileen Spinelli, "Re: Paula Danziger," e-mail to author, October 17, 2004.

2. Personal interview with Sam Danziger, "Re: Paula Danziger," November 2, 2004.

3. Ibid.

4. Kathleen Krull, *Presenting Paula Danziger* (New York: Twayne Publishers, 1995), p. 11.

5. Bill Valadares, "When Life Gives You Lemons, Don't Swallow the Pits," *Montclair Alumni Life*, Fall 2002, <http://www.montclair.edu/pages/alumnilife/alumnilifefall02/features2.html> (March 30, 2005).

6. "Paula Danziger," *KidsReads.com*, 1998, <http://www.kidsreads.com/authors/au-danziger-paula.asp> (March 17, 2005).

7. Kelly M. Halls, "Danziger Tribute," *Smartwriters.com*, n.d., <http://www.smartwriters.com/index.2ts?page=danzigerfarewell> (March 30, 2005).

8. Krull, p. 3.

9. Struckel Katie Brogan, "Writing for Kids With Judy Blume," *WritersDigest.com*, n.d., <http://www.writersdigest.com> (November 23, 2004).

10. Paula Danziger, *The Cat Ate My Gymsuit* (New York: The Putnam and Grosset Group, 1998), p. 2.

11. Krull, p. 17.
12. Ibid.
13. Personal interview with Bruce Coville, August 1, 2004.
14. Krull, p. 20.

Chapter 2. A Writer Is Born

1. Personal interview with Barry Danziger, "Re: Paula Danziger," February 2, 2005.
2. Kathleen Krull, *Presenting Paula Danziger* (New York: Twayne Publishers, 1995), p.1
3. Ibid., photo insert.
4. Ibid., p. 4.
5. Personal interview with Barry Danziger, "Re: Paula Danziger," February 2, 2005.
6. Ibid.
7. Krull, p. 4.
8. Barry Danziger, "Re: Paula Danziger." Personal interview. 2 Feb. 2005.
9. Alice Cary, "Amber Brown Goes Forth," *BookPage.com*, 1996, <http://www. bookpage. com/9602bp/childrens/ pauladanziger.html> (December 5, 2005).
10. "Learn About Bulimia," *Mama's Health.com*, n.d., <http://www.mamashealth.com/ bulimia.asp> (December 5, 2005).
11. Ibid.
12. Krull, p. 5.
13. Personal interview with Barry Danziger, "Re: Paula Danziger," February 2, 2005.
14. Krull. p. 6.

15. "Paula Danziger: Children's and Teen Book Author," n.d., <http://www.gwinnettpl.org/biobit/Danziger2004.htm> (April 2, 2005).

16. Krull, p. 2.

17. Bill Valadares, "When Life Gives You Lemons, Don't Swallow the Pits," *Montclair Alumni Life*, Fall 2002, <http://www.montclair.edu/pages/alumnilife/alumnilifefall02/features2.html> (March 30, 2005).

18. Krull, p. 8.

19. Alice Cary, "Amber Brown Goes Forth," *BookPage.com*, 1996, <http://www.bookpage.com/9602bp/childrens/pauladanziger.html> (December 5, 2005).

20. Ibid.

21. "All About Paula Danziger," Penguin Putnam, n.d., <http://www.penguinputnam.com/static/packages/us/yreaders/amberbrown/aapd.html> (March 17, 2005).

Chapter 3. A Believable Character

1. "Paula Danziger," *KidsReads.com*, 1998. <http://www.kidsreads.com/authors/au-danziger-paula.asp> (March 17, 2005).

2. Diane Telgen, *Contemporary Author: Paula Danziger. Thomson Gale*. January 1, 2004, vol. 132, p. 121.

3. Paula Danziger, *The Cat Ate My Gymsuit*. (New York: The Putnam and Grosset Group, 1998), p. 1.

4. Kathleen Krull, *Presenting Paula Danziger* (New York: Twayne Publishers, 1995), p. 29.
5. Personal interview with Sam Danziger, "Re: Paula Danziger." November 2, 2004.
6. Krull, p. 24.
7. Danziger, *The Cat Ate My Gymsuit*, p. 51.
8. "Scholastic Author and Books, Paula Danziger Biography," *Scholastic.com*, n.d., <http://www2.scholastic.com/teachers/ authorsandbooks/authorstudies/ authorstudies.jhtml> (August 25, 2004).
9. Krull, p. 27.
10. Paula Danziger, *There's a Bat in Bunk Five*, (New York: The Putnam and Grosset Group, 1998), end page.
11. Ibid., p. 4.
12. Ibid.
13. Krull, p. 33.
14. Danziger, *There's a Bat in Bunk Five* (New York: The Putman and Grosset Group, 1998), p. 84.
15. Ibid., p. 85.
16. *English Journal*, November 1984, pp. 24–27.
17. Diane Telgen, *Contemporary Author: Paula Danziger*. Thomson Gale. January 1, 2004, vol.132, p.123.
18. Danziger. *There's a Bat in Bunk Five*, p. 150.
19. Ibid.

Chapter 4. Real Life in Fiction

1. Personal interview with Sam Danziger, "Re: Paula Danziger," November 2, 2004.
2. "Paula Danziger," *KidsReads.com*, 1998, <http://www.kidsreads.com/authors/au-danziger-paula.asp> (March 17, 2005).
3. "Paula Danziger," *Teen Reads.com*, 2005, <http://www.teenreads.com/authors/au-danziger-paula.asp> (March 17, 2005).
4. Kathleen Krull, *Presenting Paula Danziger* (New York: Twayne Publishers, 1995), p. 41.
5. Paula Danziger, *The Pistachio Prescription* (New York: Penguin Putnam Books, 1998), p. 2.
6. Ibid., end page.
7. Krull, pp. 40–41.
8. Danziger, *The Pistachio Prescription*, end page.
9. Krull, p. 42.
10. Paula Danziger, *Can You Sue Your Parents For Malpractice?* (New York: The Putnam Grosset Group, 1998), p. 3.
11. Krull, p. 44.
12. Ibid., p. 46.
13. Danziger, *Divorce Express*, (New York: The Putnam and Grosset Group, 1998), end page.
14. "Paula Danziger," *Teenreads.com*, 2005, <http://www.teenreads.com/authors/au-danziger-paula.asp> (March 17, 2005).
15. Krull, p. 53.

16. Danziger, *Divorce Express*, p. 148.
17. Krull, p. 54.
18. Ibid., p. 56.
19. Ibid.
20. *Authors and Artists for Young Adults*, vol. 4 (Farmington Hills, Mich.: Gale Group, 1990), pp. 73–80.

Chapter 5. Outer Space, New York, and London

1. "Paula as Traveler," *Scholastic.com*, 1996–2005, <http://www.scholastic.com/titles/paula/traveler.htm> (December 5, 2005).
2. Kathleen Krull, *Presenting Paula Danziger* (New York: Twayne Publishers, 1995), p. 57.
3. Phyllis Graves, "This Place Has No Atmosphere," Creekwood Middle School, Kingwood, Texas, *School Library Journal*, 1986, <http://www.amazon.com/> (April 1, 2005).
4. Krull, p. 60.
5. Ibid., p. 61.
6. Phyllis Graves, "This Place Has No Atmosphere."
7. Krull, p. 59.
8. "Paula as Traveler."
9. Paula Danziger, *Remember Me to Harold Square* (New York: Penguin Putnam Books For Young Readers, 1987), p. 8.
10. Krull, p. 63.
11. Personal interview with Carrie Danziger, "Re: Paula Danziger," March 22, 2005.

12. Ibid.

13. Alice Cary, "Amber Brown Goes Forth," *BookPage.com*, 1996, <http://www. bookpage.com/9602bp/childrens/ pauladanziger.html> (December 5, 2005).

14. Ibid.

15. Ibid.

16. Personal interview with Carrie Danziger, "Re: Paula Danziger," March 22, 2005.

17. Bill Valadares, "When Life Gives You Lemons, Don't Swallow the Pits," *Montclair Alumni Life*, Fall 2002, <http://www. montclair.edu/pages/alumnilife/ alumnilifefall02/features2.html> (March 30, 2005.

18. Julia Eccleshare, "Paula Danziger," *The Guardian*, July 14, 2004, <http://books. guardian.co.uk.html> (April 1, 2005).

19. Personal interview with Carrie Danziger, "Re: Paula Danziger," March 22, 2005.

20. Ibid.

21. Ibid.

Chapter 6. Books for Boys

1. Personal interview with Sam Danziger, "Re: Paula Danziger," November 2, 2004.

2. Ibid.

3. Paula Danziger, *Everybody Else's Parents Said Yes*. (New York: The Putnam Grosset Group, 1998), pp. 23–24.

4. Personal interview with Sam Danziger, "Re: Paula Danziger." November 2, 2004.

5. Ibid.

6. Personal interview with Barry Danziger, "Re: Paula Danziger." May 9, 2005.

7. Danziger, *Everybody Else's Parents Said Yes*, p. 20.

8. Ibid., Acknowledgments.

9. Personal Interview with Sam Danziger, "Re: Paula Danziger." November 2, 2004.

10. Kathleen Krull, *Presenting Paula Danziger* (New York: Twayne Publishers, 1995), p. 74.

11. Personal interview with Sam Danziger, "Re: Paula Danziger," November 2, 2004.

12. Krull, p. 77.

13. Personal interview with Sam Danziger, "Re: Paula Danziger." November 2, 2004.

14. Ibid.

Chapter 7. Collaboration

1. "Paula Danziger Remembered," *Publishers Weekly*, September 6, 2004.

2. Lynda B. Comerford, "A True Test of Friendship." *Publishers Weekly*, March 9, 1998: pp.1–2, <http://www. publishersweekly.com> (March 1, 2005).

3. Ibid.

4. Ibid.

5. NPR Interview, *P.S. Longer Letter Later*, July 12, 1998, <http://www.npr.org/ templates/story/story.php?storyId= 1001183> (April 1, 2005).

6. Ibid.

7. "The Authors—Paula Danziger and Ann M. Martin," *Stories from the Web*, Birmingham Library and Information Sources, 2001, <http://hosted.ukoln.ac.uk/stories/stories/danziger/snailmail/email.htm> (March 25, 2005).

8. Comerford, "A True Test of Friendship."

9. Ibid.

10. Ibid.

11. Paula Danziger, and Ann Martin, *P.S. Longer Letter Later* (New York: Scholastic Inc., 1998), p. 1.

12. "The Authors—Paula Danziger and Ann M. Martin."

13. NPR interview, *P.S. Longer Letter Later*.

14. Personal Interview with Bruce Coville, August 1, 2004.

15. NPR Interview. *P.S. Longer Letter Later*.

16. Paula Danziger and Ann M. Martin, "P.S. Longer Letter Later: A Novel in Letters," *Scholastic.com*, n.d., <http://www.scholastic.com/titles/pslongerletter/longletter.htm> (September 28, 2005).

17. "The Authors—Paula Danziger and Ann M. Martin."

18. Paula Danziger and Ann Martin, *Snail Mail No More* (New York: Scholastic Inc., 1998), p. 307.

19. Paula Danziger, *United Tates of America* (New York: Full Cast Audio, CD-Rom, 2002).

20. Ibid.

21. Ibid.

22. Ibid.

23. Ibid.

Chapter 8. Danziger's Legacy

1. Personal interview with Barry Danziger, "Re: Paula Danziger," May 9, 2005.
2. Ibid.
3. Personal interview with Carrie Danziger, "Re: Paula Danziger," February 23 2005.
4. Ibid.
5. Ibid.
6. Personal interview with Barry Danziger, "Re: Paula Danziger," July 28, 2004.
7. Personal interview with Bruce Coville, August 1, 2004.
8. "Paula Danziger Remembered," *Publishers Weekly*, September 6, 2004.
9. Robert Sabuda, "Remembering Paula Danziger," *Robertsabuda.com*, <http://www.robertsabuda.com/whatsnew.asp> (March 30, 2005).
10. "Paula Danziger Remembered," *Publishers Weekly*.
11. Ibid.
12. "Remembering Paula," *The Society of Children's Book Writers and Illustrators*, <www.scbwi.org> (March 30, 2005).
13. "Paula Danziger," *KidsReads.com*, 1998, <http://www.Kidsreads.com/authors/au-danziger-paula.asp> March 17, 2005.

In Her Own Words

1. Kathleen Krull, *Presenting Paula Danziger* (New York: Twayne Publishers, 1995), p. 6.

2. Ibid., p. 2.
3. "Paula Danziger: Children's and Teen Book Author" n.d., <http://www.gwinnettpl.org/biobit/Danziger2004.htm> (April 2, 2005).
4. *All About Paula Danziger*, Penguin Putnam, n.d., <http://www.penguinputnam.com/static/packages/us/yreaders/amberbrown/aapd.html> (March 17, 2005).
5. Krull, p. 77.
6. Personal Interview with Sam Danziger, "Re: Paula Danziger," February 23, 2005.
7. "Paula Danziger," *KidsReads.com*, 1998, <http://www.kidsreads.com/authors/au-danziger-paula.asp> (March 17, 2005).
8. Kelly M. Halls, "Danziger Tribute," *Smartwriters.com*, n.d., <http://www.smartwriters.com/index.2ts?page=danzigerfarewell> (March 17, 2005).
9. Krull, p. 3.
10. Bill Valadares, "When Life Gives You Lemons, Don't Swallow the Pits." *Montclair Alumni Life*, Fall 2002, <http://montclair.edu/pages/alumnilife/alumnilifefall02/features2.html> (March 30, 2005).
11. "Paula Danziger," *KidsReads.com*.
12. Krull, p. 44.
13. "Paula Danziger," *Read In*, 1998, <http://www.reading.org/authors/archives/1998/> (April 1, 2005).
14. Alice Cary, "Amber Brown Goes Forth," *BookPage.com*, 1996, <http://www.bookpage.com/9602bp/childrens/pauladanziger.html> (December 5, 2005).

15. Krull, p. 27.

16. *Authors and Artists for Young Adults*, vol. 4 (Farmington Hills, Mich.: Gale Group, 1990), pp. 73–80.

17. "Paula Danziger," *TeenReads.com*, 2005, <http://www.teenreads.com/authors/au-danziger-paula.asp> (March 17, 2005).

18. Krull, p. 57.

19. NPR Interview, *P.S. Longer Letter Later*, July 12, 1998, <http://www.npr.org/templates/story/story.php?storyId=1001183> (April 1, 2005).

20. Krull, p. 20.

21. Paula Danziger, *There's a Bat in Bunk Five* (New York: The Putnam and Grosset Group, 1998), end page.

22. Diane Telgen, *Contemporary Author: Paula Danziger*. Thomson Gale. January 1, 2004, vol. 132, p. 123.

Glossary

acid reflux—A burning sensation in the stomach caused by acid in the stomach. The acid moves up out of the stomach toward the esophagus.

acute respiratory distress syndrome (ARDS)— Respiratory failure in adults or children caused when one or both lungs fail. Pneumonia, chest trauma, and infection can cause ARDS.

autobiographical—A story about a person by the person.

bulimia—An eating disorder, common especially among young women of normal or nearly normal weight, that is characterized by episodic binge eating and followed by feelings of guilt, depression, and self-condemnation.

collaborate—To work together.

dysfunctional—Unable to function normally.

flamboyant—Excessively ornamental.

holistic medicine—An approach to medical care that includes all aspects of a person's health.

hypochondriac—A person who is always afraid of getting ill.

interracial—Involving different races.

metaphor—A figure of speech in which a word or phrase that ordinarily designates one thing is used to designate another, thus making a comparison.

plot—The story that is told in a novel, movie, book.

sequel—A continuation of a story, often a second book.

Selected
Works & Awards

Major Works

1974 *The Cat Ate My Gymsuit*

1979 *Can You Sue Your Parents for Malpractice?*

1978 *The Pistachio Prescription*

1980 *There's a Bat in Bunk Five*

1984 *The Divorce Express*

1986 *This Place Has No Atmosphere*

1987 *Remember Me to Harold Square*

1989 *Everyone Else's Parents Said Yes*

1990 *Make Like a Tree and Leave*

1991 *Earth to Matthew*

1992 *Not for a Billion Gazillion Dollars*

1994 *Thames Doesn't Rhyme with James*

1998 *P.S. Longer Letter Later: A Novel In Letters*, Paula Danziger and Ann M. Martin

1999 *Snail Mail No More*, Paula Danziger and Ann M. Martin

2002 *United Tates of America*

Awards

New Jersey Institute of Technology Award, and Young Reader Medal nomination, California Reading Association, both 1976.

Massachusetts Children's Book Award, first runner-up, 1977, winner, 1979.

Child Study Association of America's Children's Books of the Year citation, 1978, **Massachusetts Children's Book Award**, Education Department of Salem State College, 1979.

Nene Award, Hawaii Association of School Librarians, and the **Hawaii Library Association**, 1980, all for *The Cat Ate My Gymsuit*.

California Young Reader Medal nomination, 1981.

Arizona Young Reader Award, 1983, for *The Pistachio Prescription*.

Children's Choice Award, International Reading Association and the Children's Book Council, 1979, for *The Pistachio Prescription*, 1980, for *The Cat Ate My Gymsuit* and *Can You Sue Your Parents for Malpractice?*, 1981, for *There's a Bat in Bunk Five*, and 1983, for *The Divorce Express*.

Further Reading

Books

Campbell, Janice, and Cathy Collison. *Authors By Request: An Inside Look at Your Favorite Writers*. Hillsboro, Oreg.: Beyond Words Pub., 2002.

Hill, Christine M. *Ten Terrific Authors for Teens*. Berkeley Heights, N.J.: Enslow Publishers, Inc., 2000.

Krull, Kathleen. *Presenting Paula Danziger*. New York: Twayne Publishers, 1995.

Internet Addresses

Meet Paula Danziger
http://www.scholastic.com/titles/paula/

All About Paula Danziger
http://www.penguinputnam.com/static/packages/us/yreaders/amberbrown/aapd.html

Paula Danziger
http://www.childrenslit.com/f_danziger.html

Index